D1495377

This book was devised and produced by
Multimedia Publications (UK) Ltd

Editor: Marilyn Inglis
Production: Arnon Orbach
Design: John Strange and Associates
Picture Research: Sheila Corr

Copyright © Multimedia Publications (UK) Ltd 1984

All rights reserved. No part of this book may
be reproduced or transmitted in any form
or by any means, electronic or mechanical,
including photocopying and recording, or by
any information storage retrieval system,
without permission in writing from the
publisher and the copyright holders.

First published in the United States of America 1985 by
Gallery Books, an imprint of W. H. Smith Publishers Inc.,
112 Madison Avenue, New York, NY 10016

ISBN 0 8317 5617 9

Typeset by Flowery Typesetters Ltd

Color origination by D S Colour International Ltd, London
Printed in Italy by Sagdos

LONDON

Hugh Newbury

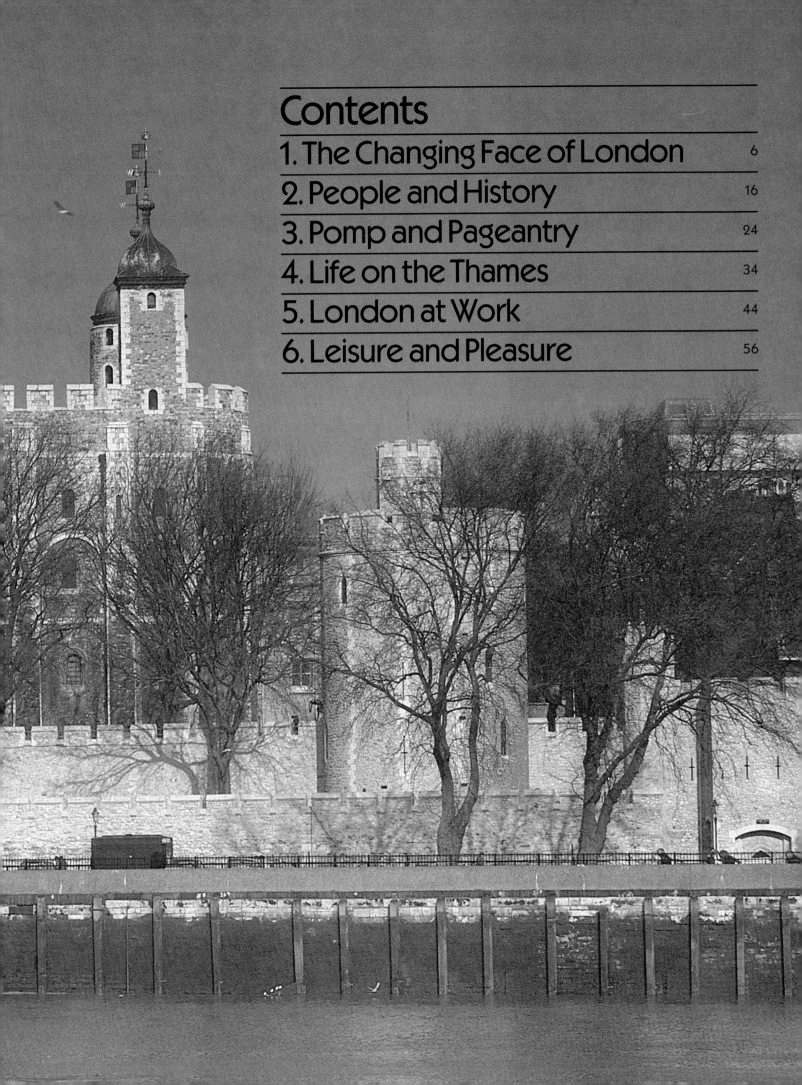

Contents

The Changing Face of London

Any first-time visitor to a city such as London comes with a few firm ideas in his hand luggage about what it is going to be like. So let's start by killing one or two of yours.

I remember arriving back in London from Paris on a beautiful crisp starlit evening and driving from the airport in a coach with other passengers. In the next seat a French couple were arguing: he thought they were in the wrong bus. "OK," he said, "if this is London, where is the fog, then?"

Thirty years ago, before the Clean Air Acts, he would have had a point. Now there is more fog in the outer suburbs, ironically often around the airport, than in the center. But the myth dies hard; all those Sherlock Holmes books and the old movies about murder in the gloom of the East End have left a picture of gas lamps flickering in the swirling mist.

The lamps have gone the same way as the fog. Other things have changed, too. The grime of centuries has been washed off many of the city's buildings; perhaps it never seemed worth doing before. New steel and glass buildings have turned parts of London into just another modern city.

Some changes seem to mark a decline; London is no longer the world's largest city nor, as surprisingly it was until a few years ago, the world's largest port. But then the numbers of visitors to London, both business people and tourists, have increased enormously; seven million overseas visitors now come to London every year.

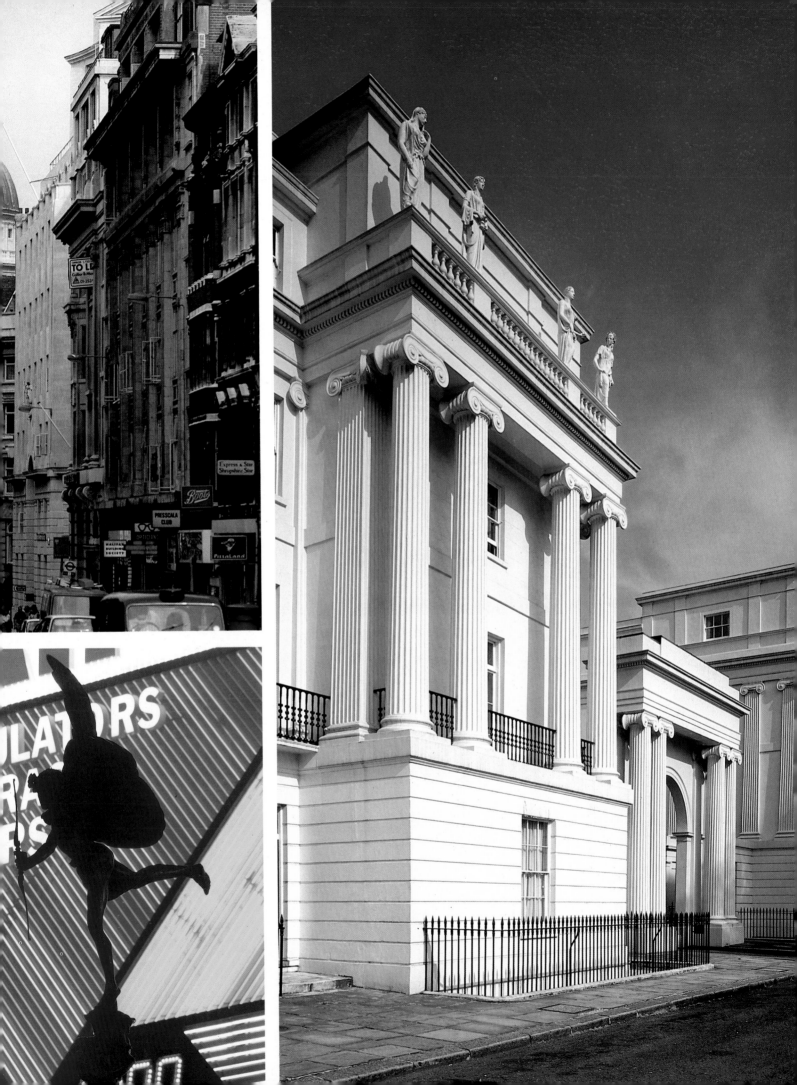

Of course some of the mental images of London are still as true as ever they were. Nowhere else in the world can you see historic ceremonial carried out with such assurance and perfection. The State Opening of Parliament, Trooping the Colour, the daily Changing of the Guard at Buckingham Palace, even the rare royal wedding or coronation seem to be part of the fabric of London, just as much a facet of the Londoner's life as the tall red buses and the unique taxis.

And of course it is the Londoners themselves who are London. They work there and eat, sleep, drink and amuse themselves there. They have their own language that "foreigners" from Sussex or Yorkshire do not understand. In London they have everything anyone could want. There is no need ever to leave the city, and until this century very few of them ever did. Few enough even left their own small part of it, their "patch". Like the inhabitants of any capital city in the world, they are impatient, but tolerant, quickwitted, cheerful, tough without being hard, with a deep well of kindness and loyalty to their fellow Londoners. And they accept without question that they live in the greatest city in the world. They would stare at you in polite amazement if you tried to tell them of a greater one. Of course, New York has skyscrapers, Paris is romantic, Rome is more ancient, Athens is more ancient still. But London is the greatest because it is theirs.

Previous page, top left One of the four dials of Big Ben. Its chimes are heard all over the globe via the BBC's World Service and, during World War II, were a symbol of hope for the people of occupied Europe.

Previous page, bottom left A London taxi. Newcomers to London sometimes laugh at its old-fashioned look, but not when they have seen one do a U-turn in a narrow street.

Previous page, bottom center If you want to ask the way from one of London's calm policemen, you should address him as "Constable" or "Sergeant" or, best of all, "Officer".

Previous page, top center Looking down Fleet Street towards the dome of St Paul's.

Previous page, bottom right The statue of Eros, the Greek god of love called Cupid by the Romans, silhouetted against the flashing signs in the middle of Piccadilly Circus.

Previous page, far right Cumberland Terrace in Regent's Park. John Nash's marvelous classical composition was built in 1826-7.

Top left Staple Inn (often called Staples Inn), in Holborn. The street front dates back to Tudor times, though the whole building was reconstructed in 1937. A German bomb destroyed the hall, with its stained glass and fine hammerbeam roof, in 1944.

Bottom left The magnificent Tudor palace of Hampton Court, near London to the west. The warm red brick is pierced by many windows, showing that in peaceful Tudor days the battlements and moat were only for show, not for defense.

Right The sumptuous Baroque interior of Sir Christopher Wren's masterpiece, St Paul's Cathedral. Built after the destruction of the old cathedral in the Great Fire of 1666, it cost £850,000, paid for by subscriptions and a tax on sea-borne coal.

Below The Albert Memorial, seen here with the Royal Albert Hall behind, was built in 1872 a few hundred yards from the site of Prince Albert's brainchild, the Great Exhibition of 1851. The Memorial is one of the peaks of Victorian art, but today we need not be too solemn about its elaborate piety.

It is also the capital of the people who gave the world its most widely spoken language. (More people may speak Chinese, but its influence is not so universal.) This is a great advantage for visitors from North America and the Commonwealth countries. However strange London may seem at first, at least the people speak no more oddly than they do in some parts of the United States. Visitors may even catch themselves forgetting for a moment that they are abroad, particularly when another myth has been squashed: that the English are taciturn. It just is not so, as you may quickly find out if you want. They may hide behind their newspapers and seem to avoid conversation, but they will chat happily if you talk to them. They are not so volatile as the Italians or the Greeks, perhaps, but not far short sometimes; you have only to ease your way through a street market in the East End to have all your illusions about the reserved English shattered.

If you really want to get on well with a Londoner (or with a Parisian or a New Yorker), try being quietly appreciative of his city. At first sight he may seem blasé about it all. But don't be fooled. Visitors quickly spot that in London history is never far below the surface, and Londoners, deeply proud of their city, feel themselves a part of its history – a continuous and continuing story stretching back 2000 years, of struggle, of poverty and riches, of desperate defense against one or another invader, above all a strong feeling that, sharing the city with their sovereign and their Parliament, they are at the very center of English history too.

Far left, facing page Perhaps the ghost of Charles Dickens stalks, notebook in hand, down this narrow alley only a few yards from the bright lights.

Top, facing page The Golden Boy of Cock Lane, Smithfield. This street was the scene of a famous real-life ghost story in 1762.

Bottom, facing page A little street leading to Streatley Place, near Hampstead Heath, one of the few places in London where you can still see cobbles.

This page Cheerful window boxes lend color to the dry offices of the lawyers in Gray's Inn.

11

Top On the Victoria Embankment, near Big Ben, stands this memorial to an earlier Queen. Boadicea (or Boudicca) ruled the Iceni, a people living to the north-east of London, who in AD 61 mounted a fearsome rebellion against the Romans. According to legend, she rode into battle in a chariot with scythes attached to the wheels. Certainly the Iceni sacked several towns, including London, before the Romans defeated them and captured Boudicca alive.

Far left The figure of Justice on top of the Old Bailey, the famous Central Criminal Court where so many spectacular criminals have faced their accusers.

Near left This fine sphinx is one of a pair that guard the Egyptian obelisk known as Cleopatra's needle, though it has nothing to do with her. The original contractor mistakenly mounted the sphinxes so that they faced towards the obelisk, instead of away from it. The companion obelisk is in New York.

Bottom One of the most recognizable buildings in the world – the Houses of Parliament. This is the place that Guy Fawkes tried to blow up, and the source of laws, opinions and statutes which have held sway all over the world. Newly elected Members of Parliament enter its portals with a sense of awe; members of the House of Lords are secure in the knowledge that their place there is assured for the rest of their lives.

Right The top few floors of the Post Office Tower, near Tottenham Court Road. It provides a tall platform for microwave links as part of the telephone service. An IRA bomb closed the revolving restaurant, the highest in England.

Below Not all of London is steeped in history. This building, with its reflecting glass panels to prevent overheating in the sunshine, is in the Euston Road.

Right Even the ancient City of London has its share of new buildings, mostly on land efficiently cleared by German bombers during the Blitz of 1940-1. This is the new headquarters of the National Westminster Bank.

2
People and History

It is not true, of course – London is not the center of English history. It has not even always been the capital of the country. Colchester was the Roman provincial capital, and Winchester was the capital of Alfred's kingdom. But London has been the dominant city since the Norman conqueror William I rode across London bridge and had himself crowned in Westminster Abbey.

There is a curious neatness about English history; it divides into 500-year chunks. Each period starts with a violent seizure of power and a time of strong rule, which brings prosperity. This is followed by increasing unrest and eventually chaos with, at the end of the 500-year period, another violent upheaval. The Romans, arriving in the first century, declined gradually until the Saxons took over around

AD 500. The growing turmoil of the Danish invasions ended with the Norman conquest in the eleventh century. The slow decline of law and order in the next five hundred years culminated in the Wars of the Roses from which the strong Tudors emerged as victors in the sixteenth century. Shall we see a repeat of history in the twentyfirst century?

London was founded in the first century when the Romans came up the Thames looking for a good crossing point. They saw it was the first place with reasonably hard dry land on each side: the country between there and the estuary was mostly marsh. They set up an efficient ferry service and then a bridge made of boats lashed together, with a few huts at each end for the bureaucrats. The settlement needed to be supplied, so they made a deep water quay

and, since these were dangerous times, they eventually built a wall round the houses on the north side of the river – but not before the vigorous Boadicea, Queen of the Iceni, had sacked the place.

The wall defended a substantial town, with the houses of rich merchants and officials, public buildings, a forum and all the trappings of Roman civilization. Outside the wall and its gates there grew up a huddle of squalid hovels where the indigenous people lived. This difference between the "city" inside the walls and the rest of London outside them has lasted to this day: the "City" of London, with its boundaries little changed since Roman times, is quite separate from the sprawl of London beyond. It has its own jealously guarded administration and privileges, and even now the sovereign formally seeks permission from the Lord Mayor before entering the City. (Nowadays the Lord Mayor politely offers the Queen the keys of the City, but in the Middle Ages things were not always so courteously done.)

Roman order and solid government lasted only until the fourth century. Increasing pressure from the Saxons, coming across from the continent, brought final collapse. The Saxon settlements in their turn were menaced by the Danes, sailing up the river in their longships, and it was not until the Norman conquest of England in the eleventh century that William I's strong rule brought a period of settled order to London.

This was the time when fortunes were made from the wool industry and other trades and crafts, with the result that merchants often became richer than the

The Great Fire of London as seen by a Dutch artist. Old St Paul's is in the background. Note the buildings on London Bridge. Pepys saw "Everybody endeavoring to remove their goods, and flinging them into the river or bringing them into lighters that lay off; poor people staying in their houses as long as till the very fire touched them ..."

king. These merchants took good care that they ran the City: not for nothing is the town hall of the City called the Guildhall, after the trade and craft guilds set up by the merchants to defend their monopolies. Their offices, as now, were in the City, but their houses were almost always outside the walls, in the green fields and spinneys to the north and west.

The king, too, lived outside, in the separate City of Westminster, where he had a palace next to the Abbey. It was here, in Westminster Hall, that the Parliament met to discuss whatever the king permitted them to discuss. Universal democracy was centuries away, but at least the infant representative council was allowed to grow until in the seventeenth century it came to fully responsible adulthood.

Significantly the law courts are also outside the City. The old Common Law, dating back to Saxon times, still formed the basis of the English law until Henry II set up a parallel, but much more efficient "King's Bench" in the twelfth century. Since then the two have existed side by side in England. The parliamentary and legal systems, begun in London, were refined and developed over the centuries and were eventually taken around the world by English administrators. And the headquarters of both in London are still outside the City.

Of course London life was not always smooth. There were rebellions, disasters such as floods, fires and plagues, and there was a great deal of crime. Pirates were always a menace: John Stow, the

Below A detail from an engraving, probably by J. Kip, printed and sold by I. Smith in Exeter Change in about 1720, shows the London skyline created by Wren when he rebuilt London's churches after the Great Fire.

Above The Tower of London, from a late fifteenth-century book of poetry written by the Duke of Orleans while he was a prisoner there (he can be seen actually writing them). There is a fine view of the old London Bridge, with its buildings and the massive piers separated by narrow arches.

Above Archaeologists taking advantage of site clearance in the City of London to dig up and record yet more of London's past. The site director is explaining to the Lord Mayor the excavation of a Roman drain. This runs through the Roman warehouse which has been excavated in Pudding Lane.

Elizabethan historian of London, writes, "In the year 1216, the Londoners sending out a navy, took 95 ships of pirates and sea robbers." Executions were commonplace, and the prisons were some of the worst in Europe. Newgate, which was built in the remains of a Roman fort, was not fully rebuilt until 1780!

But London seems to have been a rumbustious, vigorous sort of place. William Fitzstephen, writing in the twelfth century, says: "In the holidays all the summer the youths are exercised in leaping, dancing, shooting, wrestling, casting the stone, and practising their shields; the maidens … dance as long as they can well see … When the great fen is frozen, many young men play upon the ice … one sits down, many hand in hand to draw him, and one slipping on a sudden, all fall together; some tie bones to their feet and … do slide as swiftly as a bird." And there was the theater (Shakespeare himself might be appearing), or failing all else there were always some executions to watch.

And all the while London was becoming more and more prosperous. After the Great Fire of 1666 there was a rush of sharp businessmen to do the rebuilding. Wren cornered the market in City churches, but there was a lot of speculative building to be done too. Squares and terraces were built for the newly rich gentry and merchants, and London spread and sprawled along the river. The vast expansion of trade lasted until the rise of German and American industrial power in the late nineteenth century. By then London, the center of England's imperial might, was the world's dominant city – in trade, finance, political power – and remained so for half a century more.

Left The Central Lobby of the House of Lords The Palace of Westminster, where the Lords and Commons sit, dates back to well before the Norman conquest in 1066, but after a disastrous fire in 1834 it was completely rebuilt in the new Victorian Gothic style.

Top right The House of Commons was destroyed again in the Blitz of 1941 and was rebuilt after the war, when the Churchill Arch was constructed from stones damaged in the bombing. The green chair seen through the arch is the Speaker's.

Bottom right Westminster Hall, with its marvelous hammerbeam roof. It is said to be the largest unsupported wooden roof in the world. Some famous people have been tried here: William Wallace, the Scottish hero, in 1305; Sir Thomas More in 1535; Guy Fawkes and his fellow conspirators in 1605; the Earl of Stafford in 1640; and Charles I in 1649.

One final test had to be faced in World War II: the Blitz of September 1940 to May 1941. It was impossible to defend the huge mass of London, 35 miles wide and 20 miles deep, from Hitler's bombers. Their attacks just had to be endured. People, even Londoners, have forgotten that 20 000 civilians were killed and another 25 000 wounded in the London Blitz. There were some horrific tragedies: 450 people in West Ham, bombed out of their houses one night in September 1940, were given shelter in a school. The next night a direct hit on the school killed every one of them. There were to be hundreds of smaller tragedies and thousands of acts of heroism, mostly unrecorded, before the astonishingly good-humored fortitude of the Londoners beat the bombers.

St Paul's cathedral incredibly survived the holocaust and became a symbol of London's endurance. A famous picture taken at the time showed the cross on top of the dome reaching up through the smoke and flames of the devastation all around. For many older people that photograph is their deepest and most enduring image of London.

Above Yeomen Warders or "Beefeaters" parade at the Tower of London in their Tudor uniforms.

Below The Speaker processes behind the mace at the State Opening of Parliament.

Right The exterior of the Guild Hall

Bottom Westminster Abbey from the south-west, seen under a blanket of snow. The original abbey was destroyed by the Danes. The present church dates from the second half of the thirteenth century, except for Henry VII's chapel with its miraculous fan vaulting, and the west towers added by Wren and Hawksmore in the middle of the eighteenth century. The interior has been overwhelmed by the addition of ornate tombs of the great and famous, turning the quiet church into a sort of museum. Some are so large that the original stonework has had to be hacked away to accommodate them.

Pomp and Pageantry

Seeing the crowds at some colorful piece of ceremonial, one is tempted to ask whether it is not just a performance put on specially for the tourists.

Certainly the spectators are not discouraged! But there is always an ancient purpose, sometimes half forgotten, and nearly always a modern one too.

For instance, in the eighteenth century it was noticed that new ambassadors in London, going to be presented to the sovereign, were sometimes so poor that they could not afford their own carriages. Occasionally they might even arrive at the palace on foot, wringing wet from a storm, and have to be dried out before they could be presented. It was no doubt felt that this reflected on the dignity not only of the ambassadors themselves and their countries, but also of the monarch who would have to welcome a sneezing and bedraggled individual standing in a growing puddle on the red carpet. So to this day one of the royal carriages is always sent to collect all new ambassadors and take them safely to the palace, whether they can afford their own large limousine or not. It is a gesture that, in levelling all differences between the richest and poorest countries, is perhaps even more relevant in the twentieth century than it has ever been.

Royal Horse Artillery firing a Royal Salute in Hyde Park to mark the Queen's birthday.

Above A Grenadier guardsman on parade. His bearskin is copied from the headgear worn by the French Guards at the battle of Waterloo in 1815 when they were defeated by the British army under Wellington. The emblem on his collar is a flaming grenade.

Below The nightly Ceremony of the Keys in the Tower of London. The sergeant and privates escort the Chief Yeoman Warder on his rounds as, with considerable pomp and circumstance, he locks the various entrances.

Opposite page The most impressive parade in London's calendar is Trooping the Colour. Each year one of the battalions of the Guards has the honor of parading its standard before the Sovereign, seen here on the leading horse inspecting the troops.

Some ceremonial has been adapted to the spirit of the times. The coronation of Queen Elizabeth II in 1953 was based on earlier ceremonies, and certainly the actual religious ritual followed very closely the coronations of all previous monarchs of which we have detailed records. The whole business was extremely long and arduous for the Queen, and she will have been glad, no doubt, that some of the surrounding ceremonial had been abandoned by Queen Victoria. The coronation banquet, for instance, was stopped after George IV's turned into a drunken orgy. Even the dignity of the coronation itself was marred when King George's estranged Queen tried in vain to get into Westminster Abbey and take part in the ceremony.

A major part of the coronation is the procession from the Palace to the Abbey and back. This is an ancient ritual. In Queen Elizabeth I's time they were called "Progresses" and were carefully organized to arouse patriotic and loyal feelings among Londoners, and so to strengthen the Queen's position against the factions plotting to overthrow her. Other less popular sovereigns hardly dared to venture out into the barrage of rotting vegetables with which the Londoners invariably greeted them.

But one procession always went down well with the crowd. The Lord Mayor's Show has been held almost every year in early winter for eight hundred years. The newly installed Lord Mayor (he is mayor only of the City of London) takes to the streets in his coach in the midst of a procession of cheerful floats. The Lord Mayor is the symbol of the independence of the City, first gained in a charter of 1215 from King John, though earlier charters exist, including one issued by William the Conqueror promising to uphold London's "laws and customs as they were in King Edward's time". So the procession proclaims to Londoners (and to any monarch who may have sinister plans) that their City is still independent and determined to stay that way. In former times it must have cost the Lord Mayor a considerable sum: he was expected to provide free food and drink for the people – on top of whatever it had cost him in bribes to get elected in the first place. (One says "he", because it was only in 1983 that a woman was first elected to the post.) Nowadays the procession is used mainly to advertize to the world some aspect of commercial life in the modern City of London.

Another ancient ceremony that takes place around the same time as the Lord Mayor's Show is the annual State Opening of Parliament, when the Queen, in state robes, drives in a carriage to Westminster to meet her Parliament. Linked with this grand occasion is another small ritual – the traditional search for explosives in the cellars of the Houses of Parliament. This dates back to 1605 when Guy Fawkes was caught trying to blow up the new King, James I, and his Parliament. And each year on 5 November throughout England children celebrate the escape of the King and Parliament with fireworks and bonfires.

One ceremony at least has had to be adapted to today's conditions. Changing the Guard at Buckingham Palace is a favorite tourist attraction, though its purpose is real enough; someone has to guard the Queen, after all. Not many years ago, the Guardsmen marched up and down outside the railings in front of the Palace. But with the increasing numbers of visitors they were always in danger of being molested by enthusiastic tourists. So they now go through their drill in the safety of the forecourt, out of reach of the crowds.

Finally we should not forget that there are many tiny ceremonies in London each year, some of which date back six or seven centuries. One is "beating the bounds", in which the choir of St Dunstan's-in-the-East walk round the boundary of the parish and beat the boundary stones with sticks, partly to check that the stones are still there and partly to make sure the choirboys remember where the boundary runs.

The earliest of these old ceremonies is probably the Quit Rent payment made at the Royal Courts of Justice at Michaelmas. It all began in 1235 when a blacksmith rented some land in Fleet Street from the king, who demanded an annual rent of six horseshoes and "sixty and one more" nails. The smithy has long since disappeared, of course, but the rent is still paid, for some reason that no one can quite remember, by the City of London. The horseshoes and nails are handed over with due ceremony to the Queen's Remembrancer – but even he has forgotten exactly why.

Left London shows the very best it can achieve in the way of pageantry for the wedding of the Prince of Wales and Lady Diana Spencer. Here is just one small, but most important, part of the vast procession which wound its way through the streets, keeping the huge crowds enthralled all the way. It was a long day of cheering, waving the Union Jack, and wishing the happy couple well.

Above Behind all the ceremony there is always a lot of hard work for some. In the Royal Mews a senior coachman polishes one of the carriages, a landau, used during state visits by foreign dignitaries, for instance, to take the Queen and her guests to Buckingham Palace on their arrival in the capital.

Below Some things are not what they seem. Bessie Martin makes crowns and all the other regalia for a London theatrical costumier.

Near right Lady Donaldson, the first woman ever to be elected Mayor of the City of London in all the eight centuries since the first Mayor. Here she is in her robes driving in the golden coach in her Show in November 1983.

Far right Aldermen's beadles in their finery. The Aldermen are the Mayor's council, and their beadles are minor officials often concerned in the past with law and order. One hopes the mace is only symbolic, and not really for defending the person of the Mayor.

Below These are the pikemen of the Honorable Artillery Company who perform various ceremonial functions in time of peace. But they are actually part-time soldiers and, less picturesquely dressed and armed, would have real duties in wartime.

Left A suitably eggy float in the Easter Parade at Battersea Park.

Below A Viking longship in the Lord Mayor's Show that accompanies the newly installed Mayor through the streets of the City of London each year.

Right Beating the bounds. The choristers of St Dunstans-in-the-East church make the round of the parish boundary once a year and beat the boundary stones, partly to make sure they have not been moved and partly to teach the choristers where the parish boundary lies.

Below Each year six young members of the Watermen's Company, one of the ancient City guilds, row a race on the Thames for Doggett's Coat and Badge. The race is over 4½ miles against the tide from Old Swan Pier at London Bridge to the Old White Swan Inn at Chelsea, now Swan House, Cheyne Walk. The prize (see page 38) was given by Thomas Doggett, a comedian at Drury Lane Theatre, in 1716.

Right Two Chelsea Pensioners take the air. These old soldiers live in the Chelsea Hospital designed by Wren in the reign of Charles II. Their uniform looks strange only to us: 200 years ago no one would have given it a second glance.

Life on the Thames

The Thames flood barrier under construction. Huge watertight gates are swung up from the bed of the river to keep exceptionally high tides from reaching London. For the first time Londoners feel safe from the danger of flooding.

Nearly every great city is built on a river which has generally played a considerable part in its growth and prosperity. London is sited where it is because the Romans found it the best place to cross the Thames, and since then the river has been a thoroughfare for goods and people not only into and out of London, but also within the city itself. It is for this reason that London stretches further along the river than away from it. Before the railways and the petrol engine, travel on land was slow and difficult: the quickest coach to Edinburgh, four hundred miles away, took six days in the 1820s, barring accidents.

But of course the river had its drawbacks. If it gave easy access to merchant ships coming up from the sea, it equally allowed enemy fleets to get right up into the heart of the capital. The Danes besieged the wretched Ethelred in London in about 994, but could get their ships no further than London bridge. Canute in 1016 dug a large trench or canal to bypass the bridge and managed to besiege London on all sides. In the seventeenth century the Dutch threatened to do the same: they actually got into Chatham harbor, near the mouth of the Thames, in 1667 and bombarded the naval dockyard.

Another problem with the river has been the danger of flooding. A combination of an exceptionally high spring tide and a strong east wind blowing up against a large flow of water coming down the river can bring disaster. Londoners hope they have now prevented this happening in the future with the new barrage which can be shut to stop the tide reaching London itself.

Disease was also a danger. All London's sewage eventually drained into the Thames, and nothing effective was done to stop the fearful stench until the middle of the nineteenth century. The Elizabethan poet Spenser wrote of "Sweet Thames", and Morris, a contemporary of Chaucer, referred to "The Clear Thames". But it was neither: poets are notoriously bad historians. At last Members of Parliament, whose new building was right on the waterside, could stand it no longer and devised some laws which cured the problem.

Later laws also cured the increasing pollution of the river. Up to the eighteenth century Thames salmon were famous. The pollution drove them out. Now, after nearly two centuries and several Acts of Parliament, young salmon are being put into the river with a real hope that they will breed there again. Already a dozen or more different species of fish can be caught.

The feature of the medieval Thames that drew the crowds was the bridge. The early one was made entirely of wood and was built on the Roman foundations of the first bridge of all. Like all the rest of London (and most other towns and cities of the time), the wooden structure made it extremely vulnerable to fire. In fact it seems to have been damaged or destroyed on average about every ten years! It is significant that other parts of England helped London in the rebuilding, which seems to show that a large area of the country depended on London bridge. At last in 1176 the Londoners decided to rebuild their bridge in stone, and it was so successfully constructed that it was only demolished in 1831.

The bridge was an ideal site for a shop, of course. Hundreds or perhaps thousands of people passed that way every day. So tall houses were built on each side of the roadway, with shops beneath. The southern end had a mill which got its power from a waterwheel turned by the river. And towards the middle there was a drawbridge so that large ships could pass through. The piers supporting the roadway and the houses were quite close together: it was obviously safer to keep the spans short. But the piers were also massive, and this had an unexpected effect. It actually restricted the flow of water so much that in a severe winter the river would freeze over. The inhabitants of London then had a new playground, and they took to it with relish. Market stalls were set up, fairs were held and all sorts of games and sports kept the people amused. They roasted oxen and had horse races on the ice, but the most spectacular must have been the coach

Above Westminster Bridge. The Embankment was built in the nineteenth century as an early attempt at flood control. In the Middle Ages it was sometimes possible to row large boats inside Westminster Hall!

Right The famous sailing ship "Cutty Sark" is in a special dry dock at Greenwich, not far from the National Maritime Museum. She was launched in 1869 and is today a powerful symbol of London's worldwide trading links.

Top, facing page The Prospect of Whitby, a well known noisy bustling riverside pub at Wapping, in London's dockland.

Bottom, facing page Traditional decoration and even pictures enliven many of the craft on the canals that connect the Thames with the industrial Midlands and North of England. Before the railways were developed in the 1830s and 1840s, canal boats were the only means of transporting heavy goods inland.

races. One year a fair was in full swing when a sudden thaw had many of the stalls floating down the river. The Thames seems not to have frozen over properly since the old bridge was pulled down.

Until 1855 the Lord Mayor's Show went part of the way by river, and it is as a thoroughfare that the Thames was most used. Samuel Pepys, the seventeenth-century diarist, was always going up and down the river by small boat. He went by river to see the great Fire of London in 1666, from which most of the people escaped by boat with as many of their goods and chattels as they could carry. A century later it seems to have been the custom for boatmen and passengers to shout insults to each other as they passed. James Boswell records that Dr Samuel Johnson, the poet, essayist and critic, once answered a passing jibe by shouting back what must be the most cumbersome insult in history: "Sir, your wife, under pretence of keeping a bawdy house, is a receiver of stolen goods." It is probably just as well for today's river travelers that the custom seems to have lapsed.

Left A winner of Doggett's Coat and Badge (see page 32) with his impressive trophy.

Below Thames barges trying to catch a shifting wind. A crowd of them can be seen nowadays only when they hold their annual race. In former times they acted as mini grain clippers, vying with each other to be the first to bring cargoes from the inland ports on the rivers of East Anglia to the great port of London.

Top right Pleasure on the river for a pair of oarsmen – and pleasure behind them on the bank in the marvelously situated Dove, a "real ale" pub at Hammersmith. No doubt the rowers will revive themselves there later.

Bottom right Some of London's docks, their job taken over by the modern container ports elsewhere, have been preserved, along with their handsome warehouses, for various other purposes, including a fine marina for small craft.

Left If you enjoy industrial archaeology, finding the roots of a country's power and wealth, then you could do worse than start in London. The world's earliest railways are here, and so too is an extensive canal system, still used and useful some two centuries later. Here, in Bethnal Green, the gas-holder seems to be puffed up with something more than just antique pride.

Below Much of the dockland area is to be redeveloped for other uses, now that the trade has gone to the new container ports around the country. But bureacracy grinds slowly, and these warehouses, perhaps Victorian or even earlier, wait to hear their fate with a lugubrious Dickensian air.

Above At Camden Lock, on the Regent's Canal, they built this graceful little bridge among the stern warehouses and industrial grime.

Below Charles II had Sir Christopher Wren build not only the Chelsea Hospital for old soldiers, but also the Greenwich Hospital for sailors too. This is the magnificent river front of the classical building, which now houses the Royal Naval College. Behind, between the domed towers, can be seen the Queen's House, built by Inigo Jones in 1616, oddly spanning the Dover Road. On the hill at the back is Greenwich Observatory, with the Prime Meridian where you can stand with one foot in each hemisphere. It was London's dominance in world trade that gave Greenwich its Prime Meridian, used in world navigation.

Above Lambeth Palace, the official residence of the Archbishop of Canterbury, head of the Anglican church, not just in Britain but throughout the world. The Palace was badly damaged in an air-raid in May 1940, and the chapel was almost completely destroyed.

London at Work

London's wealth in Roman times was centered in overseas trade. Today, 2000 years later, nothing has changed except the products in which the merchants deal.

It would not be too fanciful to say that the British Empire was founded, expanded and maintained against all opposition by the ruthless energy of London's entrepreneurs.

The Romans originally came to Britain for its grain, desperately needed for their continental empire. They also exploited its minerals – tin, iron, gold. Later, in the Middle Ages, wool was the commodity that brought the foreigners' money rolling in. Later still, with the discovery of exotic lands, spices, tea, coffee and cotton were imported, and the products of Britain's industrial revolution were exported.

This huge volume of trade led to developments in banking and finance generally, and spin-off trades such as shipbuilding and inland transport. London had the lot. The port of London, for instance, was not just a terminal for overseas shipping. It was one of the chief ports for coastal shipping, taking the imported goods to the Midlands and North of England, to Scotland and Wales, and returning with their goods for export or with food for London. But London was also a great shipbuilding center: it was only with the coming of the iron ships, more easily built close to the iron foundries and coalmines of the North and Wales, that London's industry declined. Even so, Brunel's gigantic ship the *Great Eastern* (692 feet long, displacing 32000 tons) was launched, with difficulty, at Millwall in 1858.

Another satisfied customer at the market in Berwick Street, in Soho. This area, only a few steps from the bright lights of Piccadilly Circus, is renowned for its food shops and restaurants, where you are more likely to hear Italian, French or Spanish being spoken in the streets than English.

Left "Miss Fan", a well known character in the Portobello Road junk and antiques market.

Below This sturdy Londoner is a porter in the wholesale meat market at Smithfield, established in 1614.

But, though the shipbuilding went, the port remained. It had grown with the increasing trade in the seventeenth and eighteenth centuries until the problem was how to get all the heavy goods efficiently distributed around the country. Coastal ships could not reach the manufacturing towns miles from the sea. So a network of canals was built all over England and Wales, and several important ones linked the Thames to the industrial Midlands and North. It was only the railways in the 1840s that stopped further development of the canals, though they are still used today.

Apart from shipbuilding, most of London's industry was of the lighter variety. Much of it was helped by continental workers who came to England to escape persecution at home. The London silver trade was enriched in the seventeenth century by Protestant Huguenot refugees from Catholic France. The Jewish East End tailor, with minimal, though voluble, English, has passed into folklore. Glassmaking, pottery and porcelain all benefited from trade secrets brought by European workers. In the flourishing clock trade, however, the enterprising Fromanteels, immigrants themselves, did not wait for the know-how to come to them. In 1658 one of them went to Holland and managed to "acquire" the technology behind the new-fangled pendulum, so putting London clockmaking way ahead of the world for the next 150 years. (For some reason the clock trade, and other light metalworking industries, congregated in Clerkenwell, while the silkweavers gathered in Spitalfields and the tanners in Bermondsey).

Left Portobello Road sees a brisk trade in books and pewter and ancient gramophones and many other irresistible things.

Today, inevitably, the emphasis of London business has shifted from making things to providing services for others. The City's financial institutions have always been good at buying, selling, insuring, importing, exporting, warehousing and any kind of dealing in goods and products they never see. Lloyd's of London was founded in 1687 in a coffee shop in Tower Street run by Edward Lloyd. It was far from being the first insurance organization in Europe, but it managed to combine a really efficient news service about ships, their cargoes and maritime affairs generally with the profitable business of insuring other people's risks. Today Lloyd's is still the world's center of information about the movement of every ship afloat. And its underwriters will insure anything from a racehorse to a space rocket. Even insurance companies around the world reinsure with Lloyd's the risks they have taken on, just in case.

The medieval "merchant venturer", with embroidered cloak and flamboyant hat, has become the neatly suited entrepreneur of the late twentieth century. But don't be taken in by the quiet appearance: they've been here making money for a while and reckon to be here for quite a bit more.

Right More up-market (literally) than the Portobello Road is the Burlington Arcade, running northwards from Piccadilly. Here quiet sleek sales people are only to be distinguished from the quiet sleek shoppers by the latter's bowler hats and rolled umbrellas.

Top, facing page Top people have been going to Trumper's in Curzon Street, Mayfair, since forever it seems, for a leisurely haircut and a bottle of their special stuff to put on afterwards.

Bottom, facing page If you don't feel like strolling as far as Soho, you can get some fine cheeses here in Jermyn Street.

Right The Church Bell Foundry in Whitechapel, often called the Whitechapel Bell Foundry, has been practising its craft for over four centuries. But some of the methods used today, such as fine-tuning a bell by grinding the inside, is less laborious than once it was.

Bottom left This spectacularly unspoilt shopfront and the house beyond still have their original windows and shutters. So many London houses and shops have been ruined by having modern plate glass windows, without glazing bars, inserted into graceful earlier facades.

Right A quiet still-life of bells. The Whitechapel Foundry made the bells for Big Ben, and the American Liberty Bell was first cast here in 1752.

Below This patient horse is used to standing about in all weathers while his master concludes some tricky business. Their trade, going from door to door and buying and selling anything that will earn them a profit, is called "totting".

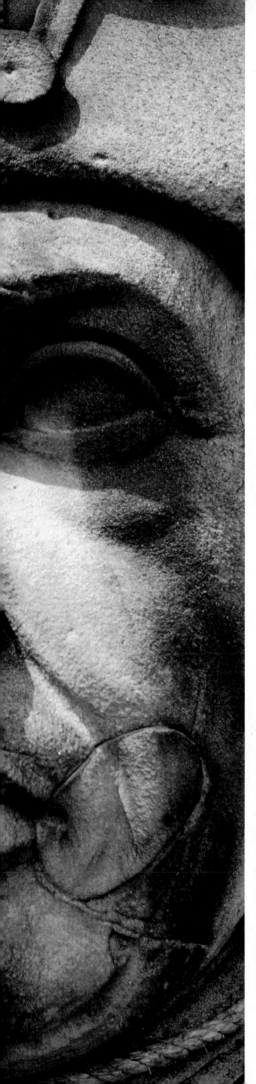

Far left Nelson stoically bears the periodic cleaning on the top of his column in Trafalgar Square. Indeed, the cleaner seems to be under more strain, as well he might, at 180 feet above the pavement.

Left This tailor has been making riding breeches in Saville Row, the summit of the trade, for well over half a century.

Below The "cooper" has every right to be cheerful in his work. He makes barrels for Young's of Wandsworth, one of the leading "real ale" breweries in England. Young's still use horse-drawn drays or carts for delivering beer: it seems it is more economic than a truck for short distances.

Left This glum crowd of City commuters look as though they are being marched off to a labor camp! A few years ago nearly all the men would have worn bowler hats, the traditional City uniform. Now there is hardly a hat of any sort to be seen.

Top right Is he buying or selling? Perhaps the price is a shade more (or less) than he would like. But this is the Stock Exchange: he must make the best of what he can get on the day.

Right Barristers have worked from Dickensian "chambers" since long before Dickens. They were hereabouts in the Middle Ages, no doubt with their names on a board at the foot of the staircase like these twentieth century ones.

Far right A critical discussion, perhaps, between barrister colleagues on the steps of the Old Chapel of the Inner Temple, one of the old Inns of Court that act as a kind of professional club for lawyers.

3
Dr JOHNSON'S BVILDINGS

Third Floor North

Mr.& Mrs.O.B.POPPLEWELL

Second Floor North

Mr.& Mrs.Maurice BERKELEY

Ground Floor North

Mr.W.J.K.MILLAR
Mr.D.R.STUCKEY
Sir Ashley BRAMALL
Mr.Thomas CONINGSBY
Mr.Peter CONI

Mr.Gerald ANGEL

Mr.John HODGSON
Miss Gayle HALLON
Mr.Nicholas PRICE

Mr.Peter BEACH
Mr Richard VAIN

6
Leisure and Pleasure

One Londoner has found time for a snooze in the sun in St James's Park.

Some visitors seem to come to London only to pursue their own hobbies. Golfers are a prime example. Naturally, if that's what turns you on, you can play golf on a different course every day of the week. There are casinos, too, that will be only too ready to have your patronage and your money.

But, since you are abroad (remember?), why not try some of the amusements that Londoners provide for themselves and which you may not have come across before. For instance, there is cricket, the national game of the English. You may want to take some advice here, to pick a game that promises some excitement even if you are not too sure about exactly what is happening. Probably a one-day match would be best: it is easier to follow the ups

and downs of the game. If you think a
one-day match sounds too long and you'd
rather try a half-day match to begin with, I
should warn you that in professional cricket
one-day games are as short as they come.
Matches between the English counties last
three days, and international matches take
five. Just be thankful you were not around
in the 1930s when there was no time limit,
and international matches sometimes
lasted for around a couple of weeks.

 If you want something rather quicker,
then you could go to the dogs, literally.
Greyhound racing is a popular sport in
England. It does not need such a large track
as horseracing, and the whole affair is
cheaper and easier to organize. And there is
still the same excitement of trying to pick
the winners.

Top Graeme Fowler produces a classic stroke for England against the West Indies at Lords. (Cricket, in case you are not quite sure.)

Bottom The London marathon, seemingly the only popular sport where there are even more participants than spectators.

One free entertainment you should not miss is Speaker's Corner, just inside Hyde Park near Marble Arch. Anyone who thinks he has anything to say can stand on a chair and hold forth. On a fine Sunday there may be a dozen people ranging from experienced preachers to members of the Flat Earth Society all trying to get their message across and dealing as best they may with the inevitable (and often witty) hecklers in the crowd. The couple of laconic policemen are there not to stop people preaching sedition and outright revolution, but just occasionally to prise apart overexcited speakers and hecklers.

Of course, you should certainly not miss some visits to the theater while you are in London. London runs two opera houses and must be one of the few cities in the world outside Germany that can mount performances of Wagner's Ring cycle using native singers. Or you may like to go talent spotting in the pop music scene and try to see who will follow the Beatles and the Rolling Stones to immortality.

Left Wimbledon has attracted stars like John McEnroe, here apparently imitating Peter Pan, and huge crowds of devotees each summer for over a century.

Below This striking shot conveys something of the competitive tensions aroused in the greyhounds at a dog track. Similar tensions can be seen among the spectators with a fortune at stake.

Then, too, you should see some English paintings while you are in London. If you do nothing else, you should go and look at the Constables, Turners and Hogarths in the Tate Gallery. There are other specialist collections you may like to see: the magnificent old arms and armor at the Tower of London, early clocks and watches at the Science Museum, including one of the earliest mechanical clocks in the world, the tennis museum at Wimbledon, the waxworks at Madame Tussauds or any one of a dozen others you can pick out of the guide books.

New pleasures are always being added. One of the latest to get established is the cheerful Notting Hill carnival, which every August brings Caribbean noise and color to the streets of London.

The justified criticism of English cooking in the past has brought little short of a revolution over the last ten years or so. The best and most expensive places were always beyond reproach, except for the cost. At the other extreme, the diners and cafés for truck drivers and other workmen were marvellous value, with plates piled with good solid tasty food. It was the restaurants and hotels between that were so unimaginative. It was generally better to find a fastfood restaurant; then at least you knew what you would get.

Top, facing page The holy of holies of intellectual London: the Reading Room of the British Library. It is one of the major joys of membership that, on asking for some rare and ancient book, one is likely to be brought a first edition. One of the most famous members was Karl Marx.

Bottom, facing page "What a remarkable hat!" Two old gentlemen contemplate each other in the Victoria and Albert Museum.

Above Inside the Liberal Club, the portraits of long dead celebrities stare coldly down on the living members. It was in just such exclusive environments that much of the politics of England (and the world) were discussed and settled over quantities of port. Now, so it is said, there is democracy, but the image of the smoke-filled room dies hard.

Right While in London you should take the opportunity to sample traditional English cooking on home ground. At Winstons Restaurant you won't find kebabs or sukiyaki – just superb roast beef, exquisite English puddings and fine English cheeses in peak condition.

Above A Pearly King and Queen in all their finery. Their spectacular dress is a sort of uniform adopted by the leaders of the street traders in the nineteenth century when they had to argue their case against the local shopkeepers who accused them of taking their business.

Above right An eel shop in Dalston. Jellied eels, with a variety of shellfish, such as whelks, have long been a popular dish in the East End of London. Amazingly, oysters were the staple diet of the poorest London people in the nineteenth century.

Right Speaker's Corner in Hyde Park, near Marble Arch. You are welcome to have a go yourself: all you need is something to stand on, a loud voice and enough repartee to deal with the inevitable hecklers. To judge by some of the speakers, it seems not to be necessary to actually have anything in particular to say.

Now the whole picture has changed. The fastfood restaurants are still there, but the rest of the middle range of places to eat have improved enormously. In particular, many pubs now go to a lot of trouble to attract customers at lunchtime with good home cooking, instead of the sandwiches and "pie and chips" that were almost universal.

The best of English cooking is probably to be had in one or two restaurants in the West End and the City, such as Simpson's Old English Restaurant in the Strand, near the Savoy Hotel. The roasts, steak and kidney pies and the puddings are superbly done. Only if you are lucky enough to be invited to one of the great London clubs may you do better – but not always. Apart from these summits, some restaurants around London specialize in English food: your restaurant guide will list them, along with Indian, Chinese, Javanese (subtle and spicy), Greek and almost anything else.

And, to drink with your steak and kidney pudding, what could be better than a glass of proper English beer. Faced with increasingly bland beers from the big breweries, lovers of real English ale banded together in the seventies to stage an astonishingly successful consumer revolution; within a few short years the Campaign for Real Ale (CAMRA) had halted the decline and you should now have little trouble in finding a traditional English pint.

So, having explored London, its magnificent buildings, majestic river, bustling crowds and picturesque corners, what better way to relax than to join Londoners themselves and fall into conversation in that most lively and friendly of English institutions – the pub.

Top The second most famous address in London: 10 Downing Street, the official residence of the Prime Minister (Buckingham Palace has an altogether more imposing entrance and no street number).

Left Strictly speaking, fish and chips is a dish from the north of England. But it is so delicious that the Londoner has quelled all his prejudices and accepted it as part of his life. You should, too, while you are in England.

Right A street theater group, at work beside the portico of St Paul's, Covent Garden, have clearly got a hold on their audience.

Below Not for sale! These luscious blooms are part of a show at the Royal Horticultural Society's hall. Flower shows – the most famous is the one at Chelsea – bring to the center of London the color and scent of the country garden.

Facing page Every August the Notting Hill Carnival takes to the streets in a riot of color. Derived from the Trinidad Carnival, it retains many of its customs. Here is the Carnival King of 1984, from Cocoyea 'mas' and Metronome Steel Orchestra, his magnificent costume paying a traditional homage to the Red Indian.

Left Like Paris's Montmartre with the Moulin Rouge, London's Soho has its Windmill Theatre complete with flashing lights and the promise of glamor within.

Right Maybe London nightlife is enough to make your hair stand on end – but if you are young and trendy, it may do it all on its own. London's Hippodrome is one place where it's all going on.

Below The last night of the Promenade Concert series is a riot – almost literally. The Royal Albert Hall audience joins in enthusiastically with the BBC Symphony Orchestra in a program of classical and patriotic music.

Right Cheerful bawdy entertainment at Aba Daba. Maybe not the place to take your maiden aunt, unless she was in vaudeville herself.

Below But you could take anyone's maiden aunt here, to the Bricklayer's Arms, for a quiet drink and a "natter". She might even get a game of darts with the locals.

Above If you brought your yacht (or even if you didn't), you can have a drink by the waterside at the Dickens Inn in the St Katherine's Dock yacht haven. The river provides some of the most interesting pubs in London.

Left The splendidly decorated front of the Sherlock Holmes pub. The Abbey National Building Society, whose head office is around the mythical 221b Baker Street, get 30 letters a day addressed to the famous detective. They gravely answer them all, saying that Mr Holmes has retired to Sussex to keep bees and declines to undertake any further investigations just now.

Major Attractions

1 Nelson's Column. In the center of Trafalgar Square, among the fountains and the pigeons, stands the mighty pillar of Nelson's column, topped by the statue of one of the greatest soldiers of English history.

2 The National Gallery. This vast art gallery houses one of the greatest collections of paintings in the world. Whichever schools of art you prefer, you are bound to find them represented here.

3 Buckingham Palace. This must be one of the most popular spots in the world for sightseers. Outside the gates you will meet tourists from all nations and, if you're lucky, you may even catch a glimpse of one of the Royal Family as they arrive or leave. Balcony appearances are reserved for special occasions.

4 Houses of Parliament. The seat of British government, this magnificent building stands in a commanding position on the very bank of the Thames. It is impossible not to catch a sense of history from its ancient, mellowed stones. Big Ben, on the eastern end of the houses, is undergoing a facelift.

5 Tower Bridge. An unmistakable silhouette on the Thames, this is the last of London's bridges before the sea. Along the bridge you will find a chimneypiece, serving the fireplace in the guardroom in the parapet.

6 The British Museum. This holds antiquities from all over the world – see the Elgin marbles, Benin bronzes, and the Reading Room, where Karl Marx researched *Das Kapital*. Wander through its labyrinthine halls and corridors and find things you never even dreamed existed.

7 The Royal Albert Hall. This is used as a venue for all manner of events – boxing, tennis, pop concerts, classical music of all types and, of course, the Proms. You may be fortunate enough to hear a choral mass performed by a chorus five hundred strong – but, in any case, it is worth a visit to see the ornate red velvet and gilt-encrusted tiers and boxes.

8 The Festival Hall. In contrast to the Royal Albert Hall, this is an auditorium of unabashed modernity where you can hear performances by the cream of international musicians. It is a part of the South Bank complex, where there are two smaller concert halls, the Hayward Gallery, a cinema and the National Theatre.

9 Lambeth Palace. This is the London home of the Archbishop of Canterbury, and has been so since it was built in the eleventh century.

10 The Victoria and Albert Museum. This beautiful museum houses exhibits ranging from costumes and furniture dating from the time of Queen Anne to modern ephemera. Particularly fine are the Islamic rooms, the musical instruments and the textiles, and you should also see the Great Bed of Ware, which is so large that 12 people could sleep in it!

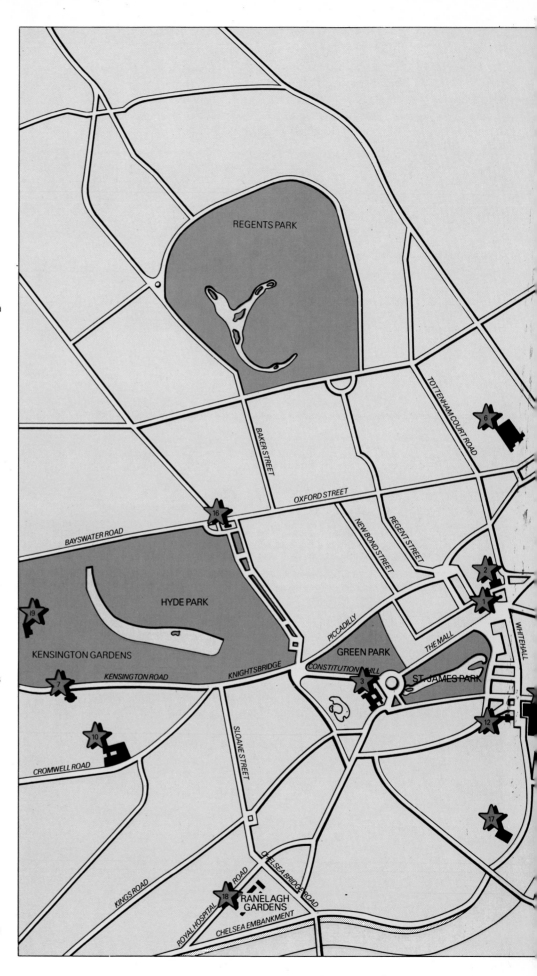

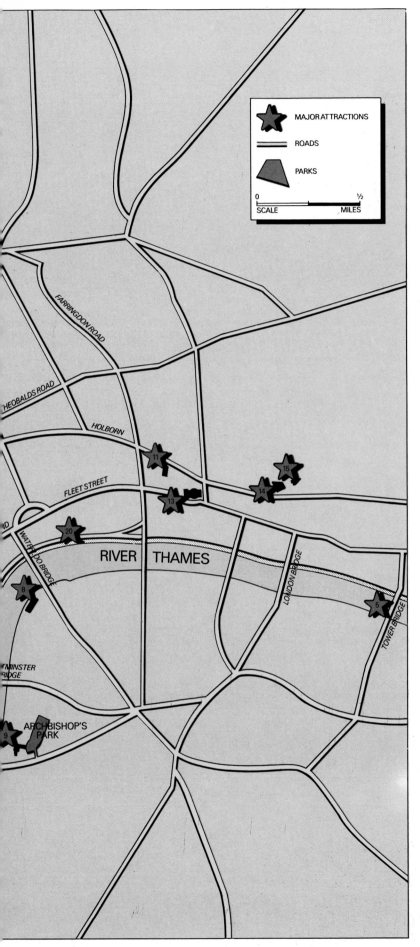

11 The Old Bailey. This majestic building has heard the most gruesome, torrid, and scandalous cases in English criminal history. Every lawyer wants to appear there; every criminal doesn't!

12 Westminster Abbey. This beautiful abbey provides the last resting place for England's kings and queens, poets and soldiers. It is largely built in gothic style, but the twin towers are eighteenth-century additions.

13 St Paul's Cathedral. The original was burnt down in the Great Fire of London, and what you see today is the work of Christopher Wren, who rebuilt so much of London after the Fire and created a skyline which remained intact over the centuries until very recently, when modern skyscrapers obscured much of it.

14 The Bank of England. The official Bank of England dates from 1694, when it was needed to provide finances for the French Wars. It was nationalized in 1946, and stores and controls the nation's gold reserves. The building dates from the late eighteenth century.

15 The Stock Exchange. From the visitor's gallery you can watch money being made on the trading floor below. Highly trained guides give informative talks, and you can also watch a documentary film.

16 Marble Arch. The Arch itself was designed by John Nash, creator of the sweeping terraces around Regent's Park, as a main gateway for Buckingham Palace. It never fulfilled this function, and stands now on the site of Tyburn, where criminals were hung, drawn and quartered before appreciative crowds.

17 The Tate Gallery. Most noted for its collection of modern art, the Tate nevertheless has paintings by Turner and the Pre-Raphaelite Brotherhood which you should not miss. It generally has a lively contemporary exhibition running.

18 Chelsea Royal Hospital. Originally built by Wren in 1682, it was added to by Robert Adam and completed by Sir John Soan. There is a statue of Charles II in the courtyard which is reputedly by Grinling Gibbons, and there is a small museum which tells the Hospital's history. There are about 400 Chelsea pensioners, recognizable by their colorful uniforms. The gardens were opened to the public in 1724, and the Chelsea Flower Show takes place here every year.

19 Kensington Palace. This is the house where, at eighteen, Queen Victoria was awakened at 6 a.m. to be told of her accession to the throne of England. It is currently the London home of the Prince and Princess of Wales.

20 _Discovery._ There are several historic ships moored on the Thames embankment, and this is the one on which Captain Scott sailed to the Antarctic in 1901.

PICTURE CREDITS

Ace Photo Agency 6 top, 14-15 **All-Sport** 58 top, 59 **Aspect Picture Library** 6 bottom left, 22 bottom
J. Bethell Photography title page, 7 right, 8 **British Tourist Authority** 6-7, 22 top, 32 top, 37 top, 39 top, 48, 60
bottom, 64 top, 68 top **Camerapix Hutchison** back cover **Bruce Coleman Ltd.** 42 top, 47 **Colorific!** 9, 29, 36
bottom, 50-51, 52-53, 63 top, 67 bottom **Daily Telegraph Colour Library** 39 bottom, 41, 46 bottom, 55 top **The
Fotomas Index** 18-19 **Robert Harding Picture Library** 13, 15, 31 top, 34-35, 42-43, 69 right **Michael Holford**
18 **Angelo Hornak** 12-13 **The Image Bank** Carol Lee 6 bottom right, Norman Perman 11 **Impact Photos** 61 top,
68 bottom **Andrew Lawson** 10 top right, 30 top right, 38 top, 49, 50 top, 51 top, 53, 62 top left, top right, 64 bottom
The Museum of London 16-17, 19 **PictureBank Photo Library** 61 bottom **The Photographers' Library** 7
bottom left, 69 left **The Photo Source** 10 bottom right, 20, 21, 23, 28, 40-41 **Rex Features** 14, 58 bottom, 60 top, 62
bottom, 63 bottom, 67 top **Spectrum Colour Library** half-title page, 12 top, 26 top, 30 bottom, 31 bottom, 32 bottom,
38 bottom, 43 top, 50 bottom, 55 bottom left **Tony Stone Photolibrary, London** contents page, 24-25, 27, 33, 36 top,
55 bottom right **Vautier-de Nanxe** 46 top **Diana Vowles** 65 **ZEFA** front cover, front endpaper, rear endpaper, 10
left, 37 bottom, 44-45, 54, 56-57, 66, 72

**Multimedia Publications (UK) Limited have endeavored to observe the legal requirements with regard
to the suppliers of photographic material.**